PHONICS FIRST A

Auditory Introduction to Phonics Skills

Elwell — Murray — Kucia

Contributors:	Merrily P. Hansen
	Royce Hargrove
Design:	Remen-Willis Design Group
Cover:	John K. Crum

ISBN: 0-8136-0233-5 Book
ISBN: 0-8136-0235-1 Chart
ISBN: 0-8136-0232-7
Printed in the United States of America

23 24   09 08 07

www.pearsonlearning.com

Level A Contents

UNIT FOUR

UNIT FIVE

UNIT SIX

Unit I

Letter Recognition

Directions: Ask the students to look at each picture pair and identify the picture on the left and on the right. Have them tell whether the pictures are alike or different.

LESSON I: Broad similarities: left to right progression

5

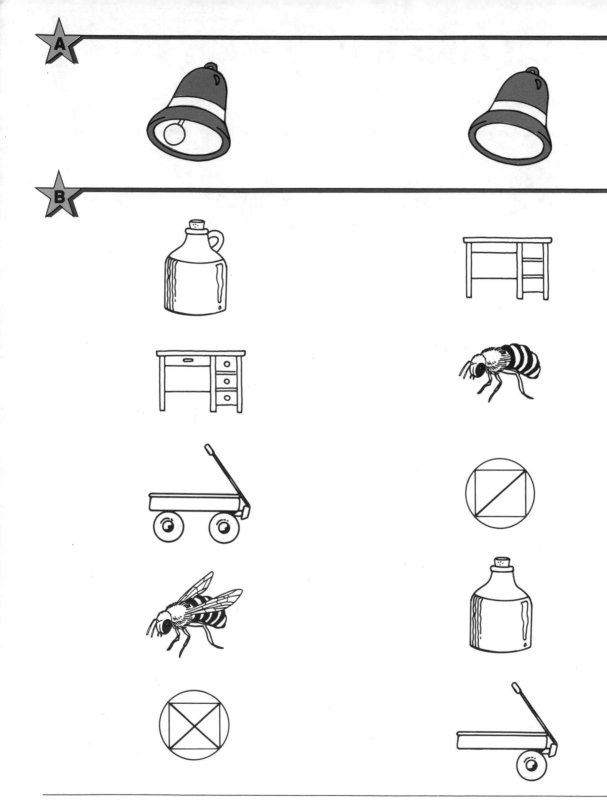

Directions: Ask the students to match similar objects on the left and right sides of the page. Have them describe what is missing from the objects on the right.

LESSON 2: Detailed similarities; noting missing parts.

Directions: Tell the students to identify each picture whose name rhymes with the first picture in the row.

WELCOME

Directions: Have the students tell whether each picture name rhymes with the word **van** or the word **cat**.

8   LESSON 4: Auditory similarities: rhyming sounds.

aa	cb	bb	ca	cc
aca	bbc	baa	cac	bcb
BB	CB	AC	CC	AA

Bb	cA	Aa	bC	cC
bA	aA	aB	bB	Cc
Cb	Bb	cC	Ac	aA

Directions: In Part B, have the students say each set of letter names and identify the letters that are alike and different. In Part C, ask students to say each letter name and identify the pairs of partner letters.

LESSON 5: Identifying **Aa**, **Bb**, **Cc**

Dd **Ee** **Ff**

ee	db	fd	dd	ce
fdf	cee	ddb	eae	dbd
EF	FF	DD	CD	EE
FFE	DDB	EFE	FDD	FEF

Fd	dD	Ce	Ee	fF
Dd	eA	eE	Ff	Bd
Ef	fF	dD	Ee	bD

Directions: In Part B, have the students say each set of letter names and identify the letters that are alike and different. In Part C, ask students to say each letter name and identify the pairs of partner letters.

LESSON 6: Identifying **Dd**, **Ee**, **Ff**

jj	ii	gj	hh	gg
ijj	ghg	iij	gjj	hbh
IE	HH	II	JJ	GG
HHF	JAJ	EGG	IIE	HBH

Ii	gG	Jg	bH	Jj
jG	Hh	iJ	Gg	iI
jJ	Ga	hH	gG	Hd

Directions: In Part B, have the students say each set of letter names and identify the letters that are alike and different. In Part C, ask students to say each letter name and identify the pairs of partner letters.

LESSON 7: Identifying **Gg**, **Hh**, **Ii**, **Jj**

11

ll	nm	kk	lk	mm
nmn	ill	mmn	khk	ann
MM	KK	IL	NN	LL
NNM	LIL	HKK	MNM	NNK

kB	Ll	Mm	nN	iL
Nn	mM	Il	Ld	kK
Nn	Li	Kk	mN	IL

Directions: In Part B, have the students say each set of letter names and identify the letters that are alike and different. In Part C, ask students to say each letter name and identify the pairs of partner letters.

LESSON 8: Identifying **Kk**, **Ll**, **Mm**, **Nn**

Aa Bb Cc Dd Ee Ff Gg
Hh Ii Jj Kk Ll Mm Nn

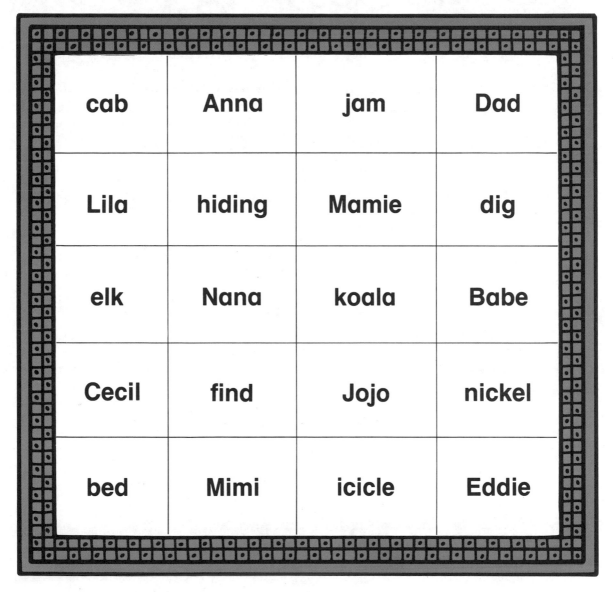

cab	Anna	jam	Dad
Lila	hiding	Mamie	dig
elk	Nana	koala	Babe
Cecil	find	Jojo	nickel
bed	Mimi	icicle	Eddie

Directions: Have the students identify the letters in the words. Do not ask them to read the words. Then ask students to identify each word that begins with a capital letter. Help them find the partner letters in these words.

LESSON 9: Reviewing **Aa**, **Bb**, **Cc**, **Dd**, **Ee**, **Ff**, **Gg**, **Hh**, **Ii**, **Jj**, **Kk**, **Ll**, **Mm**, **Nn**

pp	oo	p q	rr	pp
oao	qqg	nrr	pqp	coo
RP	OO	QO	RR	PP
OOQ	RPR	BPP	QOQ	PRP

Pq	rR	qQ	Oo	pQ
Oo	fR	aO	Rr	pP
Pd	oO	Kr	Pp	Qq

Directions: In Part B, have the students say each set of letter names and identify the letters that are alike and different. In Part C, ask students to say each letter name and identify the pairs of partner letters.

LESSON 10: Identifying **Oo**, **Pp**, **Qq**, **Rr**

B

uu	vu	tt	nu	ss
vvu	tlt	ess	uvu	ttb
VU	UU	TT	VV	TI
TTI	UVU	Gss	VNV	UUO

C

Vv	sS	uU	It	vU
Ti	vN	Tt	Uu	vV
Ss	IT	Vv	uV	tT

Directions: In Part B, have the students say each set of letter names and identify the letters that are alike and different. In Part C, ask students to say each letter name and identify the pairs of partner letters.

LESSON II: Identifying **Ss**, **Tt**, **Uu**, **Vv**

15

zz	vw	xx	yg	ww
yqy	xxz	vww	zzs	gyy
YY	WW	KX	ZZ	WV
WWV	XZX	TYY	ZSZ	YYP

C

xX	vW	Ww	zZ	Xw
Vw	yY	Sz	Xx	wW
gY	xX	wW	Zs	Yy

Directions: In Part B, have the students say each set of letter names and identify the letters that are alike and different. In Part C, ask students to say each letter name and identify the pairs of partner letters.

Oo Pp Qq Rr Ss Tt
Uu Vv Ww Xx Yy Zz

window	Robert	spot	Samson
Otto	rope	Vivian	toast
yellow	Ursula	oven	Philip
zero	Susan	vest	Roger
Titus	unit	Xerxes	prom

Directions: Have the students identify the letters in the words. Do not ask them to read the words. Tell the students to identify each word that begins with a capital letter. Help them find the partner letters in these words.

Unit 2 Consonant Sounds

Ss

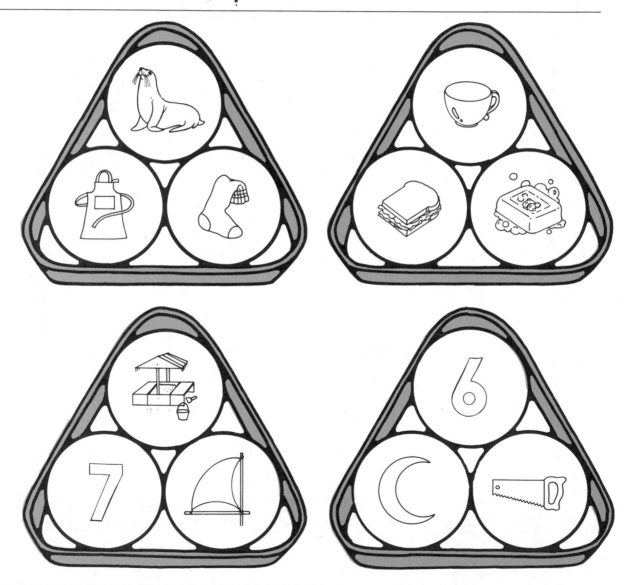

Directions: Have the students name each picture item and identify which picture names begin with the consonant sound of **S**.

18

LESSON 14: Sound of **S**

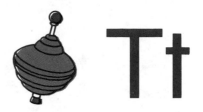

Tt

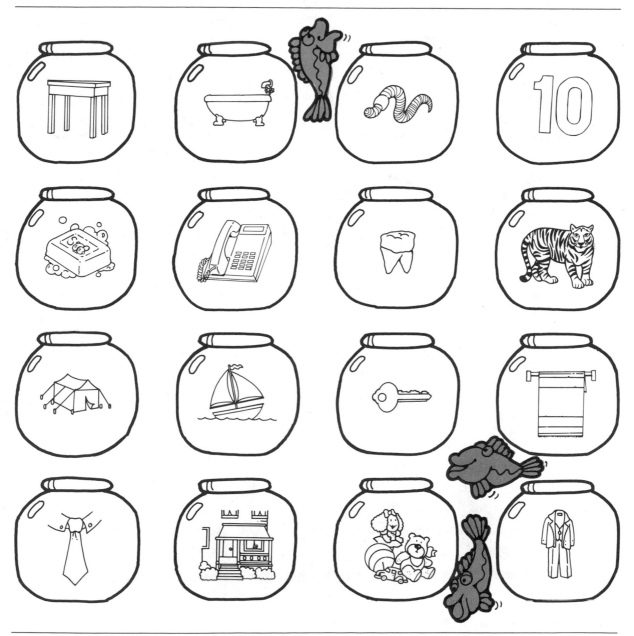

Directions: Have the students name each picture item and identify which picture names begin with the consonant sound of **T**.

Bb

Directions: Have the students name each picture item and identify which picture names begin with the consonant sound of **B**.

LESSON 16: Sound of **B**

Ss   Tt   Bb

Ss	Tt	Bb

Directions: Tell the students to look at the pictures in the first column. Have them tell whether the picture name begins or ends with the consonant sound of **S**. Repeat this procedure for the second and third columns using the consonant sound of **T** and **B**.

LESSON 17: Consonants **S**, **T**, **B**   21

Hh

Directions: Have the students name each picture item and identify which picture names begin with the consonant sound of **H**.

LESSON 18: Sound of **H**

Mm

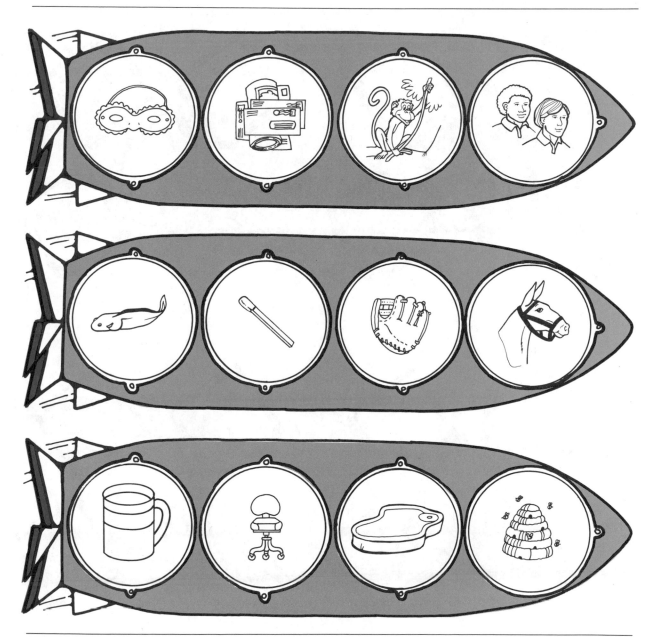

Directions: Have the students name each picture item and identify which picture names begin with the consonant sound of **M**.

Kk

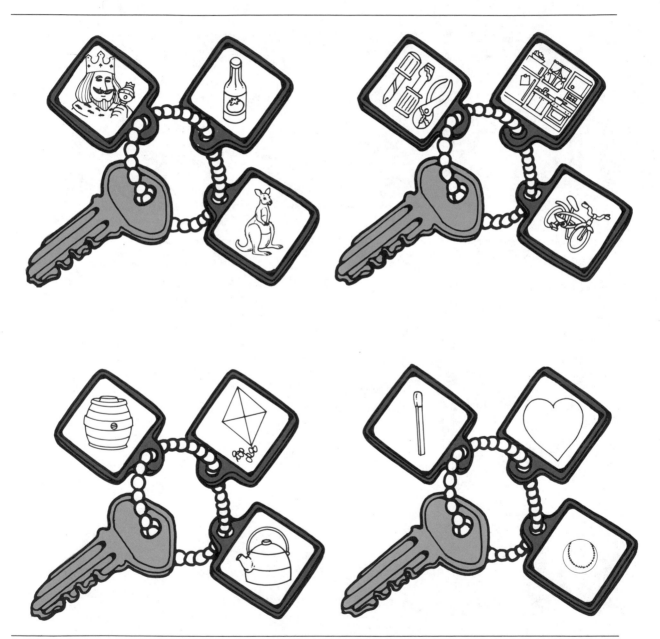

Directions: Have the students name each picture item and identify which picture names begin with the consonant sound of **K**.

LESSON 20: Sound of **K**

Hh Mm Kk

Directions: Tell the students to look at the pictures in the first column. Then have them tell whether the picture name begins or ends with the consonant sound of **H**. Repeat this procedure for the second and third columns using the consonant sound of **M** and **K**.

Ss   Bb   Mm
Tt   Hh   Kk

Directions: Have the students identify the letter that stands for the beginning sound for each picture name.

LESSON 22: Reviewing consonants **S, T, B, H, M, K**

Jj

Directions: Have the students name each picture item and identify which picture names begin with the consonant sound of **J**.

Ff

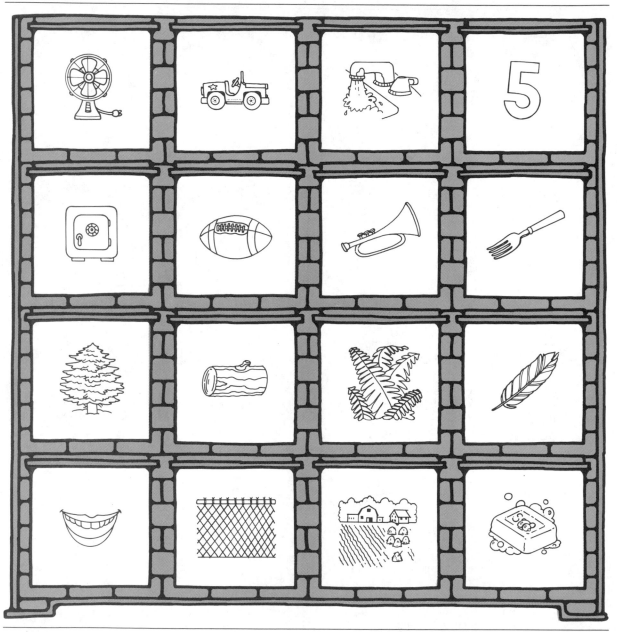

Directions: Have the students name each picture item and identify which picture names begin with the consonant of **F**.

Gg

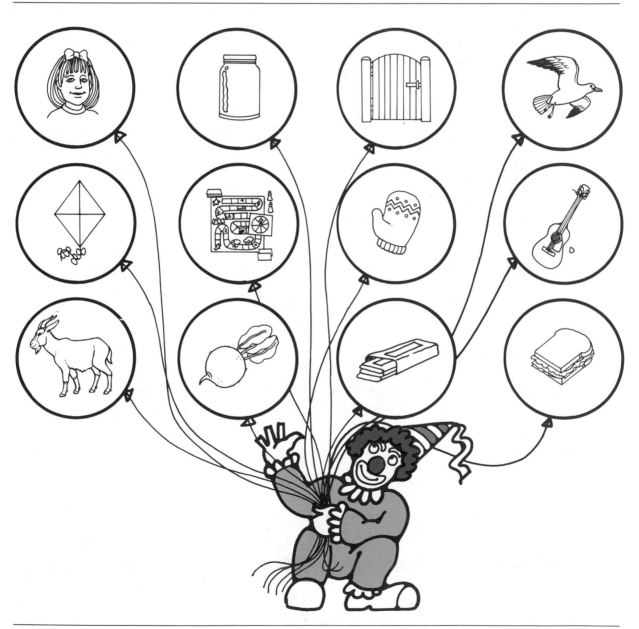

Directions: Have the students name each picture item and identify which picture names begin with the consonant sound of **G**.

Jj   Ff   Gg

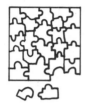		

Directions: Tell the students to look at the pictures in the first column. Have them tell whether the picture name begins or ends with the consonant sound of **J**. Repeat this procedure for the second and third column using the consonant sound of **F** and **G**.

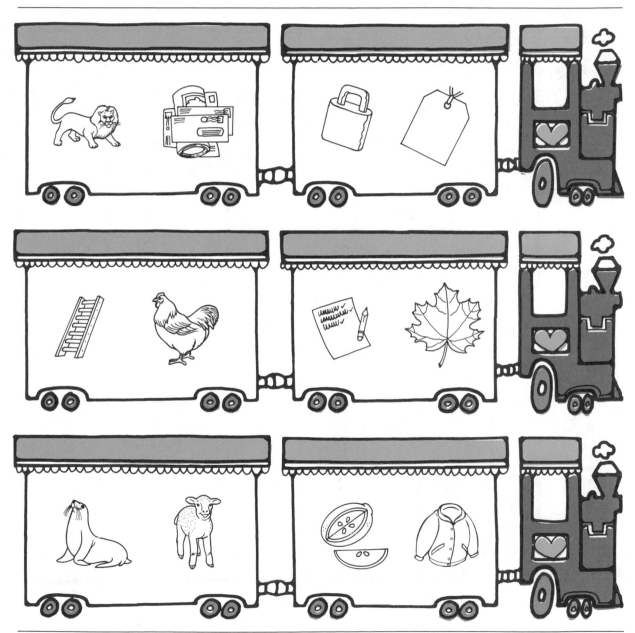

Directions: Have the students name each picture item and identify which picture names begin with the consonant sound of **L**.

Dd

Directions: Have the students name each picture item and identify which picture names begin with the consonant sound of **D**.

LESSON 28: Sound of **D**

Nn

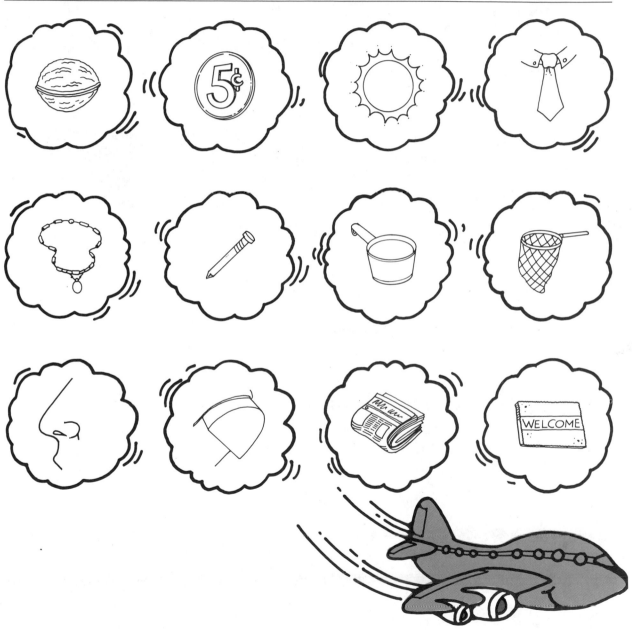

Directions: Have the students name each picture item and identify which picture names begin with the consonant sound of **N**.

Ll   Dd   Nn

Ll	Dd	Nn

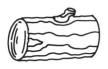	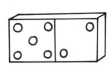	

Directions: Tell the students to look at the pictures in the first column. Have them tell whether the picture name begins or ends with the consonant sound of **L**. Repeat this procedure for the second and third columns using the consonant sound of **D** and **N**.

Ss Tt Bb Hh Mm Kk
Jj Ff Gg Ll Dd Nn

Directions: Have the students say each picture name and identify the letters that stand for the beginning and the ending sounds.

LESSON 31: Reviewing consonants **S, T, B, H, M, K, J, F, G, L, D, N**

Ww

Directions: Have the students name each picture item and identify which picture names begin with the consonant sound of **W**.

LESSON 32: Sound of **W**

Cc

Directions: Have the students name each picture item and identify which picture names begin with the consonant sound of **C**.

Rr

Directions: Have the students name each picture item and identify which picture names begin with the consonant sound of **R**.

LESSON 34: Sound of **R**.

Ll   Nn   Cc
Dd   Ww   Rr

Directions: Have the students name each picture item and identify the letter that stands for the beginning sound for each picture name.

Pp

Directions: Have the students name each picture item and identify which picture names begin with the consonant sound of **P**.

LESSON 36: Sound of **P**

 # Qq

 # Vv

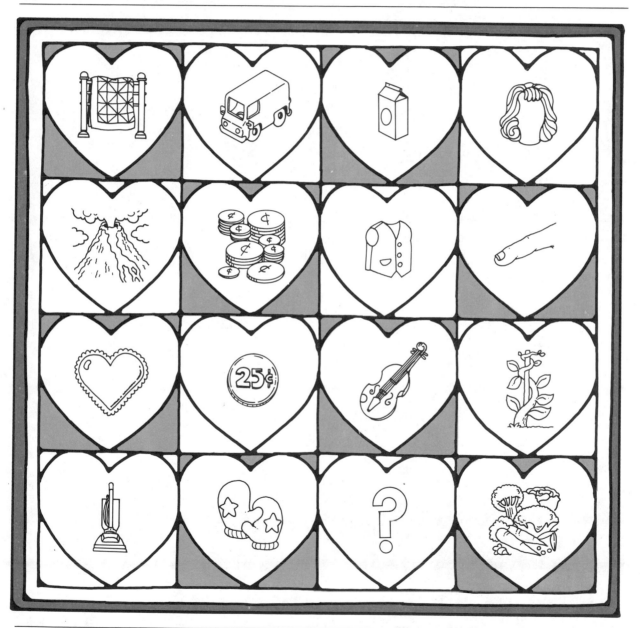

Directions: Have the students identify which picture names begin with the consonant sound of **Q** or **V**.

Ww   Rr   Qq
Cc   Pp   Vv

Directions: Have the students name each picture item and identify the letter that stands for the beginning sound for each picture name.

42   LESSON 38: Reviewing consonants **W, C, R, P, Q, V**

 **Xx**    **Yy**

Directions: Tell the students to identify which picture names end with the consonant sound of **X**. Then have them identify the picture names that begin with the consonant sound of **Y**.

Xx Yy Zz

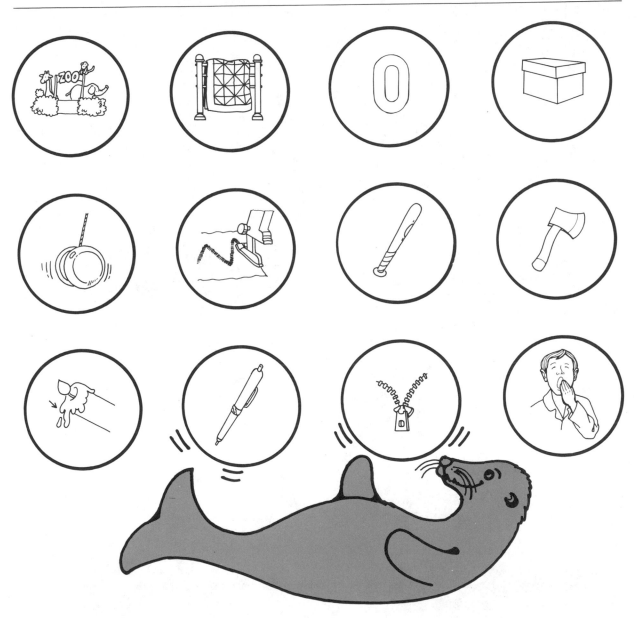

Directions: Tell the students to identify which picture names end with the consonant sound of **X**. Then have them identify which picture names begin with the consonant sound of **Y** or **Z**.

LESSON 40: Sound of **X**, **Y**, and **Z**

Ss Tt Bb Hh Mm Kk Jj
Ff Gg Ll Dd Nn Ww Cc
Rr Pp Qq Vv Xx Yy Zz

Directions: Have the students identify the letters that stand for the beginning, middle, and ending consonant sounds in each picture name.

LESSON 41: Reviewing initial, final, and medial consonants

45

Short Vowels

a	i	u	o	e
<u>a</u>nt	s<u>i</u>x	b<u>u</u>g	t<u>o</u>p	w<u>e</u>b
fan	bib	bus	pot	net
ax	pin	bud	log	nest
ham	ring	gum	dog	well
bag	lips	rug	box	desk

Directions: Have the students identify each picture name in each column. Then ask them to read aloud the letters in each word. Have the students locate the vowel in each word that matches the letter at the top of the column.

Directions: Have the students say the name of each picture as they slide down the hill to blend the sounds.

LESSON 43: Consonant-vowel-consonant blending

47

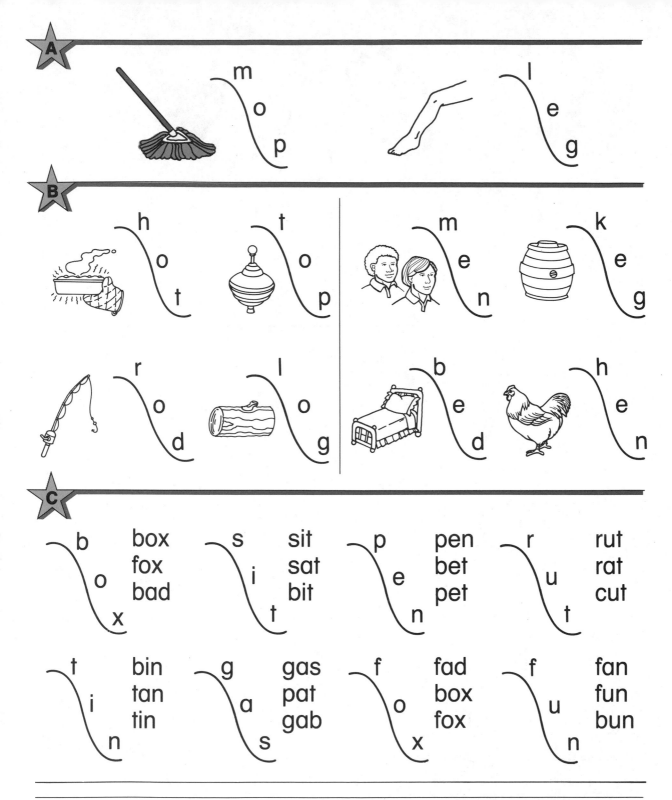

A

m
o
p

l
e
g

B

h
o
t

t
o
p

m
e
n

k
e
g

r
o
d

l
o
g

b
e
d

h
e
n

C

b
o
x

box
fox
bad

s
i
t

sit
sat
bit

p
e
n

pen
bet
pet

r
u
t

rut
rat
cut

t
i
n

bin
tan
tin

g
a
s

gas
pat
gab

f
o
x

fad
box
fox

f
u
n

fan
fun
bun

Directions: In Part B, have the students say the name of each picture as they slide down the hill. In Part C, help the students identify the word from the list that they make as they slide down the hill.

Directions: Have the students say the name of each picture in each box and identify each one that has the short sound of **A**. Then ask them to identify the pictures in the box that have rhyming names.

LESSON 45: Short vowel **A**.

49

<u>a</u>nt

tap　map lap　cap nap　rap	can　ran pan　man fan　Dan
bag　rag wag　tag sag　lag	hat　sat cat　bat rat　Pat
ham　jam Pam　yam ram　Sam	band　land hand　sand pans　cans

Directions: Tell the students to identify the picture name and read the words in each box. Then have them identify the word that names the picture.

A

Ann and Max ran fast.

B

1. Max sat.
2. Dad ran.
3. Dan adds.
4. Pam raps.
5. Ann sat.
6. Val naps.
7. Nat packs.
8. Sal taps.

C

1. Dad has a can.
2. Pam ran fast.
3. Tag had a bag.
4. Val can pack a hat.
5. Can Dan add fast?
6. Nat has a fat cat.
7. Sal can pass a ham.
8. Dad and Mac can pack a sack.

Directions: Have the students read aloud each sentence.

Tap, tap, tap.
Matt can rap.

Jan and Nat,
Pat a fat cat.

Pam can pass the ham.
Mac can pass the jam.

Dan has the rags.
Rax wags and wags.

Sam has a sack.
Dad can pack.

Directions: Tell students to look at each picture and read the couplet aloud. Then have them identify the words that rhyme.

Directions: Have the students say the name of each picture in the box and identify each one that has the short sound of **I**. Then have them identify the pictures in the box that have rhyming names.

b<u>i</u>b

hid	lid
Sid	bid
did	rid

sink	pink
ink	link
rink	wink

sill	fill
hill	will
dill	Jill

sit	pit
bit	fit
lit	hit

dips	tips
lips	rips
zips	hips

pigs	rigs
figs	digs
wigs	zigs

Directions: Have the students identify the picture name and read the words in each box. Then have them identify the word that names the picture.

Sid wins a big pin.

1. Tim hid.
2. Kim wins.
3. Sid sips.
4. Jim fills.
5. A pig sits.
6. Liz is ill.
7. Jill hits.
8. Bill will fix it.

1. Liz has a big mitt.
2. Kim can win six gifts.
3. Sid sips his milk.
4. Jill will fill a bag.
5. Bill fits a wig in the sink.
6. The pig sinks in the sand pit.
7. Sid packs pins in his kit.
8. Jim will fix the rip in the bib.

Directions: Have the students read each sentence aloud.

Tip, tip, tip.
The bag will rip.

Bill dips in the bin
To win a pin.

A pig in a wig
Did a fast jig.

Rick will pick.
Nick is sick.

Can Jim fit
The mitt in his kit?

Directions: Tell the students to look at each picture and read the couplet aloud. Then have them identify the words that rhyme.

 p<u>a</u>n

 p<u>i</u>n

B

1. bag	**3.** fat	**5.** ham	**7.** dad
2. big	**4.** fit	**6.** him	**8.** did
9. hid	**11.** bit	**13.** hit	**15.** fin
10. had	**12.** bat	**14.** hat	**16.** fan
17. sick	**19.** rang	**21.** lips	**23.** last
18. sack	**20.** ring	**22.** laps	**24.** list

C

t___p	p___t	l___ps	f___n
z___g	b___t	w___g	b___g
s___nk	l___mp	p___ck	f___st

Directions: Tell the students to read aloud the word pairs in Part B. In Part C, have the students make two words by supplying the missing vowels A and I. Then ask them to use the words they make in sentences.

LESSON 53: Reviewing short vowels **A** and **I**

57

Directions: Have the students say the name of each picture in the box and identify each one that has the short sound of **U**. Then have them identify the pictures in the box that have rhyming names.

LESSON 54: Short vowel **U**

b<u>u</u>g

duck buck	nut hut
luck tuck	rut cut
puck muck	mutt cub
mug hug	rub hub
tug rug	tub cub
bug jug	sub cap
run sun	pump bump
fun bun	jump dump
rub bus	hump lump

Directions: Tell the students to identify the picture name and read the words in each box. Then have them identify the word that names the picture.

A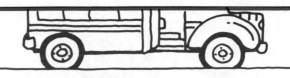

Judd huffs and puffs as he runs.

B

1. Gus will jump up.
2. Bud runs to the bus.
3. Puff tugs at the rug.
4. A bug bit Judd.
5. Pick up the nuts.
6. The pup had fun.
7. Gus just runs.
8. Judd jumps and runs.

C

1. The pup jumps in the tub.
2. Puff runs fast in the hut.
3. A bug bit the big duck.
4. Judd put a cup in the tub.
5. Bud has fun as he runs and jumps.
6. The duck is in a tub of mud.
7. Gus cut the nuts in the sack.
8. Judd put the muff and drum in the hut.

Directions: Have the students read each sentence aloud.

LESSON 56: Short vowel **U**

Bud's pup tugs
At the rugs.

Rub-a-dub-dub
Add the mugs to the tub.

Nan can jump and run.
Nan has fun in the sun.

Run, run Puff.
Pick up the muff.

The duck hid the nut
In a rut at the hut.

Directions: Tell the students to look at each picture and read the couplet aloud. Then have them identify the words that rhyme.

A

ba̲g   **bi̲g**  **bu̲g**

B

| rat | cut | mitt | tub |
| rut | cat | Matt | tab |

hat	fan	bat	ham
hit	fin	bit	him
hut	fun	but	hum

bud	tick	mud	pack
bid	tack	mad	pick
bad	tuck	mid	puck

C

b___t	c___p	t___b	r___n
h___d	b___n	c___b	c___t
m___st	j___g	h___ll	r___g

Directions: Tell the students to read the words in Part B aloud. In Part C, have them make words by supplying the missing vowel **A**, **I**, or **U**. Then ask them to use the words they make in sentences.

Directions: Have the students say the name of each picture in each box and identify each one that has the short sound of **O**. Then tell them to identify the pictures in the box that have rhyming names.

LESSON 59: Short vowel **O**

63

t<u>o</u>p

rot got cot lot dot hot	hog log bog dog jog fog
lock sock dock rock tock mock	hop pop top mop cop top
ox box fox pox tot pot	pod cod nod rod sod Tod

Directions: Tell the students to identify the picture name and read the words in each box. Then have them identify the word that names the picture.

Don adds the pop to the pot.

B

1. Mom will mop the van.

2. Tom hops fast on the rock.

3. Don has a top.

4. The tot is hot.

5. Bob has a job.

6. The doll has a sock.

7. Hop on the box.

8. The pop is hot.

1. Tom got on the rock.

2. Bob will lock up the box.

3. Don hid the pop in the sock.

4. The ox is not in the lot.

5. Ron has a cod on his rod.

6. The fox will hop off the log.

7. Lon has a job in the bus lot.

8. Mom and Dad sit on the big rock.

Directions: Have the students read each sentence aloud.

Tom will mop.
Don will hop.

Mom will jog
To the log.

Don has a rod.
Don got a cod.

The big frog
Hops on the log.

Don is hot.
Don sits on the cot.

Directions: Tell the students to look at each picture and read the couplet aloud. Then have them identify the words that rhyme.

B

lack lock	tip top	bug bog	cut cot
tock tick tack	sick sock sack	in on an	bat bit but
dog dig dug	rig rag rug	lag log lug	luck lock lick

C

___x c___p b___g	f___x c___t t___ck	r___p p___p l___ck	r___d c___b s___ck

Directions: Tell the students to read the words in Part B aloud. In Part C, have the students make words by supplying the missing vowel, **A**, **I**, **U**, or **O**. Then ask them to use the words they make in sentences.

LESSON 63: Reviewing short **A**, **I**, **U**, and **O**

Directions: Tell the students to say the name of each picture in the box and identify each one that has the short sound of **E**. Then have them identify the pictures in the box that have rhyming names.

LESSON 64: Short vowel **E**

w<u>e</u>b

pet	set	melt	felt
wet	jet	belt	pelt
let	met	bell	held

vest	best	fed	bed
west	nest	wed	led
rest	pest	red	Ted

sent	dent	pen	ten
tent	bent	hen	men
went	lent	Ben	den

Directions: Tell the students to identify the picture name and read the words in each box. Then have them identify the word that names the picture.

Ted sells vests and belts.

1. Ed fell in the web.
2. The sun sets in the west.
3. Meg fed the hen.
4. Deb is in bed.
5. Ted fed his pet.
6. The pen is red.
7. The web is wet.
8. Jed went to the left.

1. The hen is in the next pen.
2. Bev put a bell in the well.
3. Ten men got wet legs.
4. Ken sits at Meg's red desk.
5. Ned's belt is on Ted's bed.
6. The men set up nets in the pond.
7. Peg can not sell the bell with a dent.
8. Put the red quilt on Kent's bed.

Directions: Have the students read each sentence aloud.

LESSON 66: Short vowel **E**.

Ted led the hen.
Bev will add it to the pen.

The desk leg is bent.
Its top has a dent.

Ring the bell.
Ten eggs to sell.

Ted, Ned, and Fred,
Jump into bed.

Ten men get set.
Ed gets wet.

Directions: Tell the students to look at each picture and read the couplet aloud. Then have them identify the words that rhyme.

A

<u>a</u>nt

t<u>o</u>p

s<u>i</u>x

web

b<u>u</u>g

B

c___p	b___ll	t___p	t___ck
r___b	m___t	f___n	b___d
b___t	l___t	b___g	c___b
p___ck	s___ck	s___p	w___ll

C

1. The duck can not j___mp.
2. The bus is in the l___t.
3. Bill's sled is r___d.
4. The mop is in the b___x.
5. Ask Pam to pass the h___m.
6. The sun sets in the w___st.
7. Tom hit the ball with his b___t.
8. Mom has a bib on the t___t.
9. Gus adds the cups to the t___b.
10. Fix the tag on the big ink p___n.

Directions: In Part B, have the students make as many words as they can by supplying the missing short vowel. In Part C, ask them to identify the vowel that is missing in the unfinished word in each sentence. Then tell them to read the completed sentence aloud.

LESSON 68: Short vowel test

Long Vowels

cake

pail

hay

Directions: Have the students say the name of each picture and identify whether it contains the long sound of **A**.

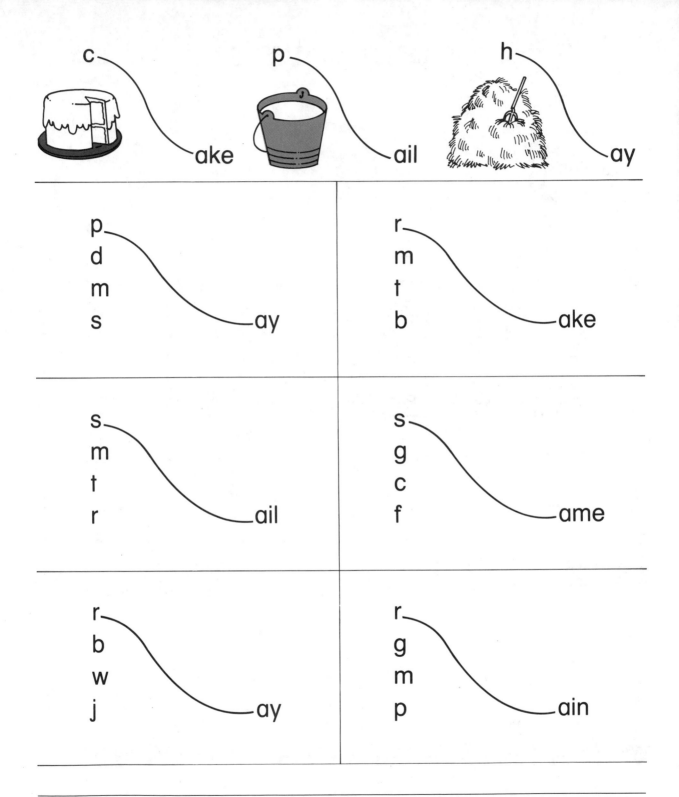

c — ake

p — ail

h — ay

p d m s — ay	r m t b — ake
s m t r — ail	s g c f — ame
r b w j — ay	r g m p — ain

Directions: Help the students form new words as they blend each beginning consonant with the other letter sounds.

c<u>a</u>k<u>e</u>

p<u>ai</u>l

h<u>ay</u>

can cane	ran rain
cape cap	ray rake
mail make	tap tame
man nail	tail tape
nap nail	cat cave
mail name	cape case

Directions: Have the students read the words in each box. Then have them identify the word that names the picture.

LESSON 71: Long vowel **A**

75

Ray can sail on the lake.

B

1. pass	3. gate	5. gave
2. lake	4. day	6. nap
7. cab	9. Jay	11. man
8. take	10. Sam	12. pail

 C

1. say	4. wake	7. ape
2. rain	5. ray	8. jam
3. game	6. Jan	9. ate
10. cane	13. pain	16. may
11. sand	14. rake	17. vase
12. had	15. Dave	18. back

Directions: Have the students read the words in each box and identify whether the vowel sound is long or short. Tell them to make a sentence for each word. Then challenge them to use all the words in each box in a sentence.

LESSON 72: Long vowel **A**

A

 cap

 cape

B

1. pan	3. ran	5. tap
2. pane	4. rain	6. tape
7. at	9. can	11. Sam
8. ate	10. cane	12. same
13. hat	15. back	17. fad
14. hate	16. bake	18. fade

C

1. Sam has on the same hat as James.
2. Ann gave the tape a tap.
3. Dave ran in the rain.
4. Pat gave the lame man a cane.
5. I will run back to bake a cake.

Directions: In Part B, have students read the word pairs and identify the vowel sound they hear in each word. Then tell them to read the sentences in Part C and identify each word with the long **A** sound.

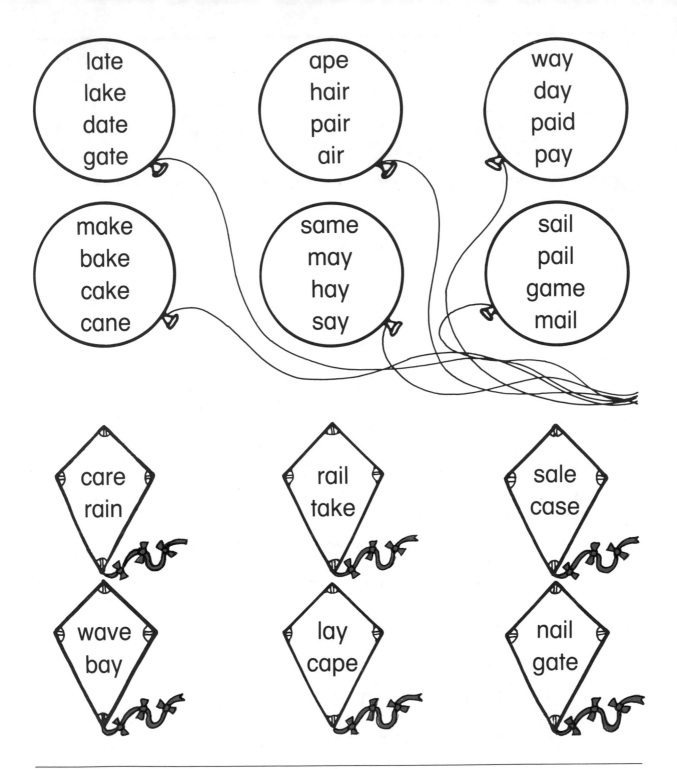

late
lake
date
gate

ape
hair
pair
air

way
day
paid
pay

make
bake
cake
cane

same
may
hay
say

sail
pail
game
mail

care
rain

rail
take

sale
case

wave
bay

lay
cape

nail
gate

Directions: Have the students say the words in each balloon and identify those that rhyme. Then ask them to say the words in the kites and use each pair in a sentence. You may wish to have students first make a sentence for each word before attempting to make a sentence using both words on the kite.

LESSON 74: Long vowel **A**

Kay made a cake in a pail.

B

1. The mail came late.

2. His name is Dave.

3. Rex has paint on his tail.

4. James ate an egg.

5. Ann and Pat made a red cape.

6. Dave came to the game with us.

7. Jane ran to the gate.

8. The rain sat in the pail.

C

1. Dan may wade in the lake.

2. Dad will pay Cass to rake.

3. Save the big nails in that box.

4. We will get a rake at the sale.

5. Did Jan wake up yet?

6. Sam will pay the man at the lake.

7. Take the mail to Dad and Sal.

8. I will get the red cap and cape.

Directions: Have the students read the sentence aloud and identify each word that has the long sound of **A**.

 kite

 tie

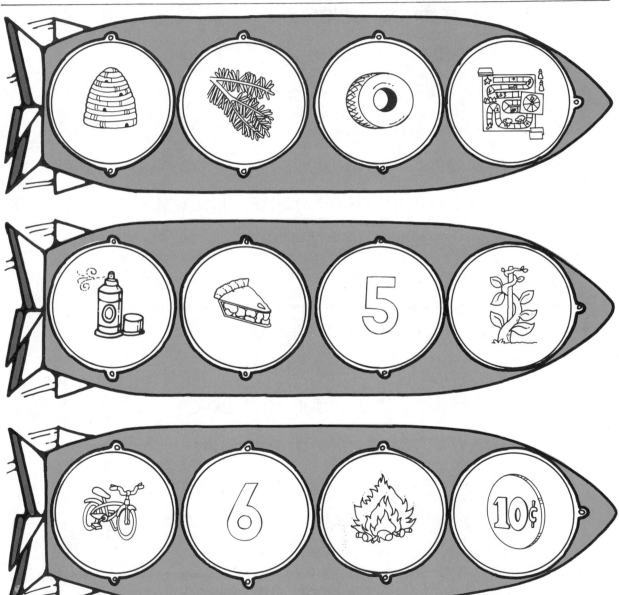

Directions: Have the students say the name of each picture and identify whether it contains the long sound of **I**.

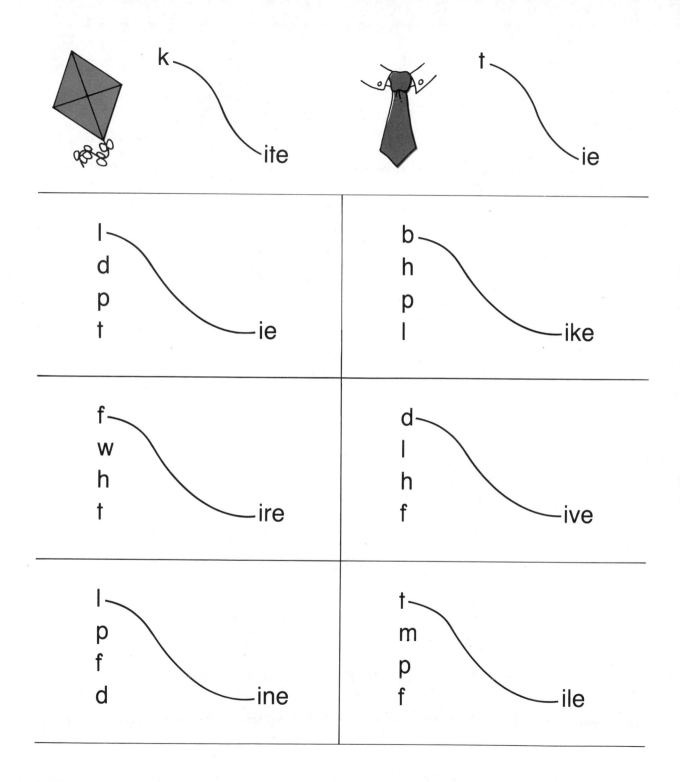

k _____ ite

t _____ ie

l d p t _____ ie	b h p l _____ ike
f w h t _____ ire	d l h f _____ ive
l p f d _____ ine	t m p f _____ ile

Directions: Help the students form new words as they blend each beginning consonant with the other letter sounds.

LESSON 77: Blending long vowel **I** words

 pin

 pine

 B

1. bit	3. kit	5. rip
2. bite	4. kite	6. ripe
7. hid	9. Tim	11. Sid
8. hide	10. time	12. side
13. dim	15. rid	17. fin
14. dime	16. ride	18. fine

 C

1. Jim has his kite at his side.
2. I like Sid's tie pin.
3. Tim will hide the rip in his bag.
4. Mike can dive in Pine Pond.
5. Kim went on a five mile hike.

Directions: In Part B, tell the students to read the word pairs and identify the vowel sound they hear in each word. Then have them read the sentences in Part C and identify each word with the long **I** sound.

LESSON 78: Long vowel **I**

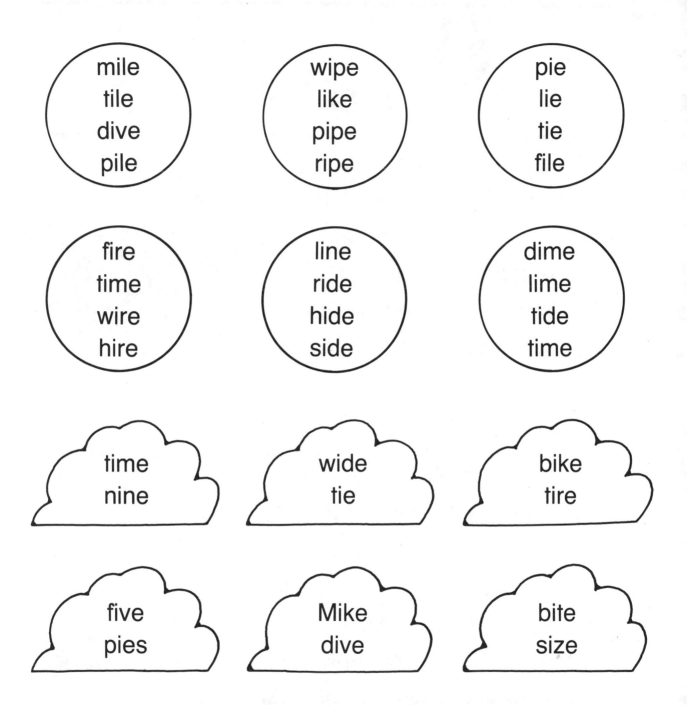

mile tile dive pile	wipe like pipe ripe	pie lie tie file
fire time wire hire	line ride hide side	dime lime tide time
time nine	wide tie	bike tire
five pies	Mike dive	bite size

Directions: Ask the students to say the words in each ball and identify those that rhyme. Then ask them to say the words in the clouds and use each pair in a sentence. You may wish to have students first make a sentence for each word before attempting a sentence using both words on a cloud.

Mike will take a bite of the lime pie.

B

1. This bike has a nail in its tire.
2. Make a wide line on the kite.
3. Tell Tim to make his dive.
4. Is that lime ripe?
5. Mike likes to ride his bike.
6. Kim gave Liz five dimes.
7. Ann made a fine lime pie.
8. We will hike in the pines.

C

1. Dale ran a mile last time.
2. Jill will wipe the sand off the wire.
3. It is not safe to make a fire in the pines.
4. I will ride a bike to the lake.
5. Put that pin on Mike's tie.
6. Pat cut the wire and the pipe.
7. Nine kids went on a five mile hike.
8. I like the big tires on the red bike.

Directions: Have the students read each sentence aloud and identify each word with a long sound of **I**.

 uniform  tube  suit

Directions: Have the students say the name of each picture and identify whether it contains the long sound of **U**.

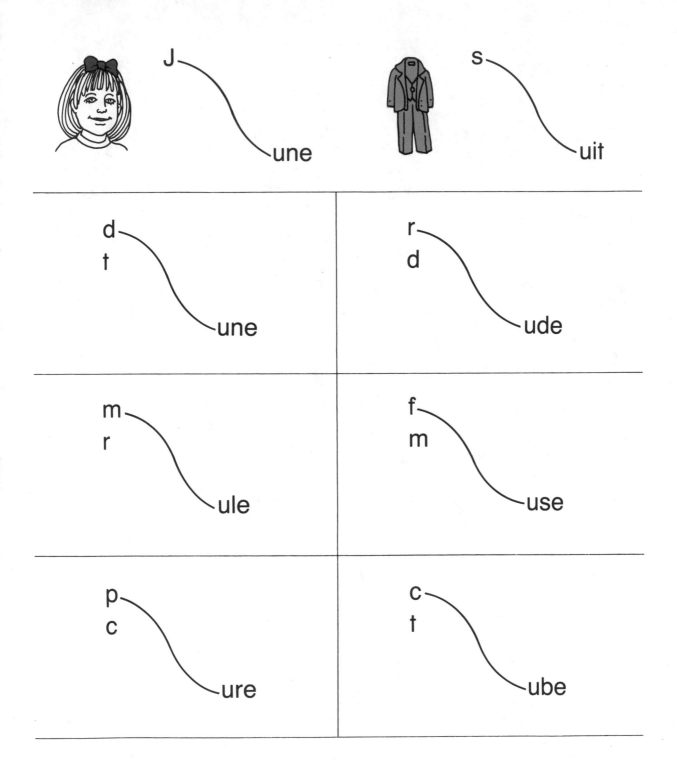

J ——— une

s ——— uit

d
t ——— une

r
d ——— ude

m
r ——— ule

f
m ——— use

p
c ——— ure

c
t ——— ube

Directions: Help the students form new words as they blend each beginning consonant with the vowel and ending consonant sounds.

The cub sits on a cube.

| 1. tune | 3. fun | 5. us |
| 2. hum | 4. Sue | 6. tube |

| 7. cute | 9. jump | 11. fuse |
| 8. pup | 10. rude | 12. pump |

1. mule	3. bus	7. cup
2. bug	4. Luke	8. tuck
3. tube	5. suit	9. rug

10. June	13. dune	16. cuff
11. fun	14. sun	17. cure
12. Luke	15. bus	18. mud

Directions: Tell the students to read each word in each box and identify whether the vowel sound is long or short. Then have them make a sentence with each word. Challenge them to use all the words in each box in a sentence.

LESSON 83: Long vowel **U**.

87

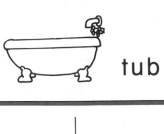 tub    tube

B

1. cut	3. cub	5. pin
2. cute	4. cube	6. pine
7. hat	9. us	11. mad
8. hate	10. use	12. made
13. luck	15. rip	17. duck
14. Luke	16. ripe	18. Duke

C

1. Sue put a tube in the tub.
2. Luke gave us a fuse to use.
3. June cut cubes of ham and cake.
4. If Duke hums, I will sing the tune.
5. The big mule has his leg in a tub.

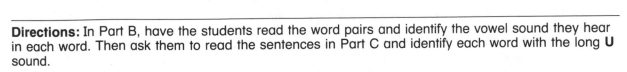

Directions: In Part B, have the students read the word pairs and identify the vowel sound they hear in each word. Then ask them to read the sentences in Part C and identify each word with the long **U** sound.

A Sue likes to use the big tube.

B
1. Luke will tell us the rules.
2. The pet mule is cute.
3. Get the fuse for Dad.
4. The glue has bad fumes.
5. Sue will ride the cute mule.
6. Tom may use the bike.
7. June likes to jump on a big tube.
8. Luke's suit is big.

C
1. Dad will use the red fuse.
2. The paste is in the tube.
3. Tom will put a cube in the pop.
4. Sue can hum a tune with Duke.
5. Luke uses the cue to hit the ball.
6. The cute pup likes the mule.
7. Jules will tell us the bus rules.
8. It is rude to say that to June.

Directions: Have the students read each sentence aloud and identify each word with the long sound of **U**.

 cake

 kite

 tube

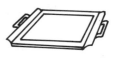

Directions: Ask the students to say the name of each picture. Then have them identify each name that contains long **A**, long **I**, or long **U**.

LESSON 86: Reviewing long **A**, **I**, and **U**

 boat

 rose

 bowl

 four

Directions: Have the students say the name of each picture and identify whether it contains the long sound of **O**.

LESSON 87: Long vowel **O**

91

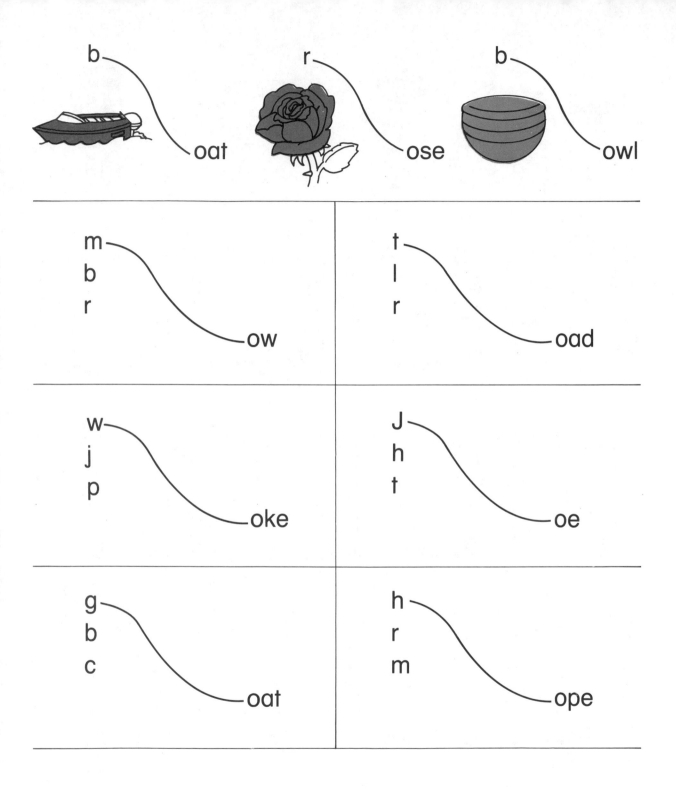

b ⌒ oat

r ⌒ ose

b ⌒ owl

m
b
r
⌒ ow

t
l
r
⌒ oad

w
j
p
⌒ oke

J
h
t
⌒ oe

g
b
c
⌒ oat

h
r
m
⌒ ope

Directions: Help the students form new words as they blend each beginning consonant with the other letter sounds.

LESSON 88: Blending long vowel **O** words

 b <u>oa</u> t
 r <u>o</u> s <u>e</u>
 b <u>ow</u> l

toad	tone	game	got
hoe	toe	goat	gain
pump	pole	rod	row
pure	pail	ride	robe
feet	face	cane	coal
four	pour	cot	cone

Directions: Tell the students to read the words in each box. Then have them identify the word that names the picture.

A

Joe will use soap and the hose on the dog.

B

1. sole	3. log	5. hope
2. hop	4. rope	6. box
7. Ron	9. pond	11. core
8. robe	10. soft	12. rode

C

1. nose	4. lost	7. coat
2. romp	5. goat	8. box
3. toe	6. fox	9. boat
10. off	13. Joan	16. pour
11. more	14. moan	17. top
12. on	15. lock	18. oats

Directions: Have the students read each word in the box and identify whether the vowel is long or short. Then ask them to make a sentence for each word. Next challenge them to use all the words in the box in a sentence.

LESSON 90: Long vowel **O**

cot

coat

B

I. rob	3. ton	5. hop
2. robe	4. tone	6. hope
7. cap	9. kit	II. not
8. cape	10. kite	12. note
13. cut	15. Lon	17. mop
14. cute	16. lone	18. mope

C

1. I hope I can hop on the road.
2. Joan will hum the notes.
3. His coat is on the cot.
4. Joe will mope if Lon has to mop.
5. The note is not for Mom.

Directions: In Part B, tell the students to read the word pairs and identify the vowel they hear in each word. Then have them read the sentences in Part C and identify each word with the long **O** sound.

Did the goat make the hole in Moe's coat?

B

1. Joe got ten votes.

2. Will Joan loan a rod to Bob?

3. Moe can pour four cups of pop.

4. The doe will go to the oats.

5. Tom will not get sore if he has to hoe.

6. No, Joe can not go in the boat.

7. Tell that joke to Bob.

8. Rose likes to jump rope.

C

1. See the big hole in Rob's coat.

2. Joe set the pail in the road.

3. Take this note to Joan and Tom.

4. Get five cakes of soap.

5. I hope Ron will take us home.

6. See the big load of hay.

7. Put the pole and jug in the boat.

8. Use the hose on the red roses.

Directions: Have the students read each sentence aloud and identify each word with a long **O** sound.

cake   kite   tube   rose

Directions: Have the students say the name of each picture. Then have them identify each name that contains the long **A**, long **I**, long **U**, or long **O** sound.

LESSON 93: Reviewing long **A**, **I**, **U**, and **O**

bee

meal

key

Directions: Have the students say the name of each picture and identify whether it contains the long sound of **E**.

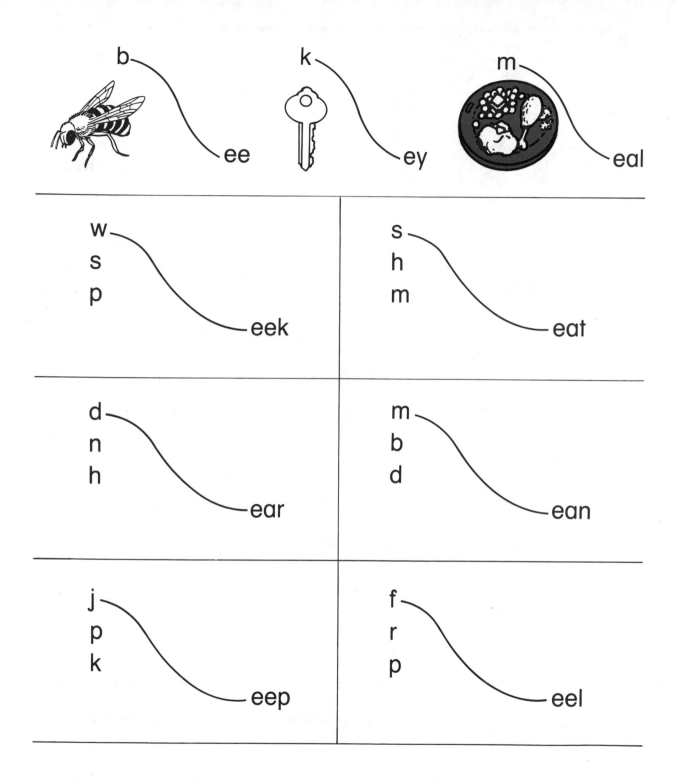

b   ee

k   ey

m   eal

w
s   eek
p

s
h   eat
m

d
n   ear
h

m
b   ean
d

j
p   eep
k

f
r   eel
p

Directions: Help the students form new words as they blend each beginning consonant with the other letter sounds.

LESSON 95: Blending long vowel **E** words

99

Meg fed the seals a big meal.

B

1. read	3. wet	5. meat
2. bed	4. leaf	6. fed
7. heat	9. meet	11. yes
8. sell	10. met	12. heal

C

1. peek	4. net	7. deep
2. egg	5. near	8. well
3. hen	6. web	9. hear
10. let	13. jeep	16. net
11. leaf	14. tent	17. seat
12. yet	15. weeds	18. need

Directions: Tell the students to read each word in the box and identify whether the vowel sound is long or short. Then have them make a sentence for each word. Next, challenge them to use all the words in each box in a sentence.

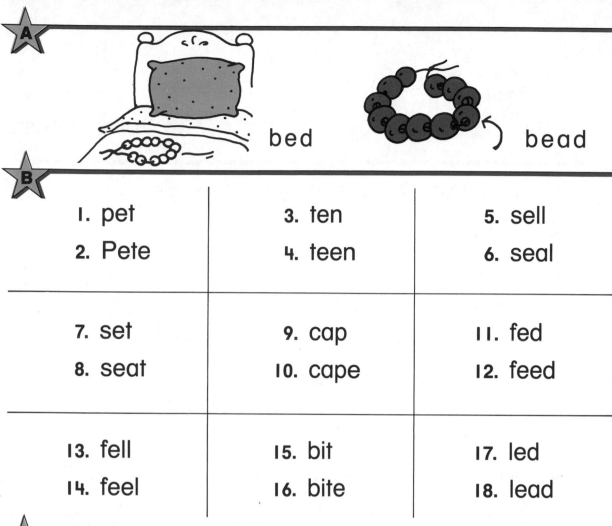

A

bed

bead

B

1. pet	3. ten	5. sell
2. Pete	4. teen	6. seal
7. set	9. cap	11. fed
8. seat	10. cape	12. feed
13. fell	15. bit	17. led
14. feel	16. bite	18. lead

C

1. Lee set the meal on his seat.
2. The men will not sell that seal.
3. The beads will be on the bed.
4. I left the keys in the jeep.
5. The queen pets ten seals.

Directions: In Part B, tell the students to read the word pairs and identify the vowel sound they hear in each word. Then have them read the sentences in Part C and identify each word with the long **E** sound.

Lee had his feet on the rear seat.

1. I can feel the heat of the fire.
2. The lake is deep and cold.
3. A big bee sat on the leaf.
4. The team will meet next week.
5. Jake likes to eat peas and beans.
6. Keep the seeds in the red bag.
7. The team leads in the game.
8. Lee likes to read in bed.

1. Keep the keys in the jeep.
2. Joan fed the deer near the tree.
3. I did not hear her say his name.
4. Can you heat up the meat for Lee?
5. Joe bet Lee he can beat Sam.
6. Set the net on Pete's seat.
7. Real seals do not eat beans and meat.
8. The team feels it can win the game.

Directions: Have the students read aloud each sentence and identify words with a long **E** sound.

cake

rose

kite

bee

tube

Directions: Ask the students to say the name of each picture. Then have them identify each name that contains a long **A**, long **I**, long **U**, long **O**, or long **E** sound.

LESSON 99: Reviewing long **A**, **I**, **U**, **O**, and **E**

r<u>i</u>de   l<u>a</u>ne

r<u>o</u>de   l<u>i</u>ne

r<u>u</u>de   l<u>o</u>ne

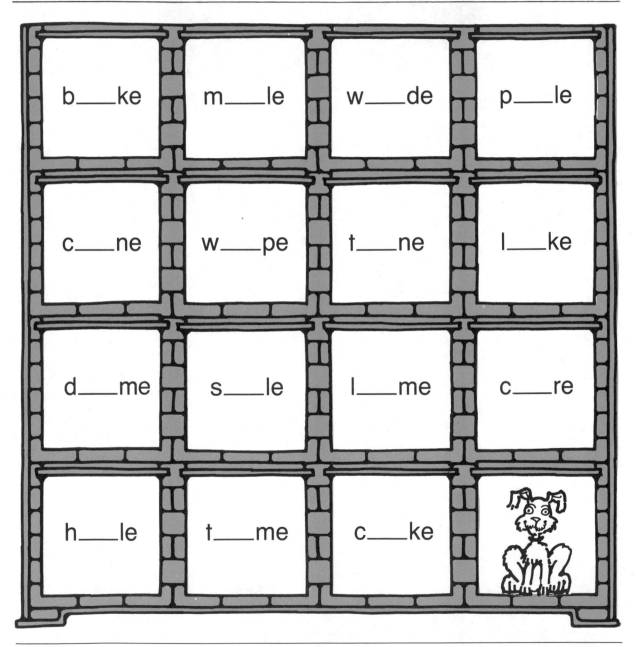

b__ke   m__le   w__de   p__le

c__ne   w__pe   t__ne   l__ke

d__me   s__le   l__me   c__re

h__le   t__me   c__ke

Directions: Ask the students to make new words by supplying correct vowels to fill the blank. Then have them use each new word they create in a sentence.

May we use a rope to tie the tube to the jeep?

B

1. week	4. door	7. may
2. life	5. low	8. cure
3. sail	6. meal	9. lie
10. dear	13. suit	16. toad
11. use	14. same	17. tune
12. loaf	15. quite	18. hear

C

1. Lee made a suit and gave it to Les.

2. We need the rope to sail the boat.

3. James put the pie and cake on the seat.

4. May I feed the mule the oats?

5. June will not hide the pail in the weeds.

Directions: In Part B, ask the students to read the words in the boxes and identify the vowel sound they hear in each word. Then have them read each sentence in Part C.

| 1. cut | 3. rid | 5. hat | 7. pet | 9. hop |
| 2. cute | 4. ride | 6. hate | 8. Pete | 10. hope |

| 11. pin | 13. at | 15. tub | 17. not | 19. us |
| 12. pine | 14. ate | 16. tube | 18. note | 20. use |

1. Can we go on a six mile hike?

2. Bob will tape the notes he has for June.

3. A bee bit Lee on his nose and on his leg.

4. The red rose is in the bud vase.

5. Sam likes to sail his raft on Pine Lake.

6. Dave can pay his way to the game.

7. Five deer came up to the camp last week.

8. It is not safe to keep meat in the sun.

9. Dad will hire Jess to put the limes in a box.

10. The game of Hide and Seek is fun if Pete is "it."

Directions: At the top of the page, ask the students to read each pair of words and identify the vowel sound they hear in each word. Then have them read each sentence at the bottom.

Consonant Blends;
Y as a Vowel

A

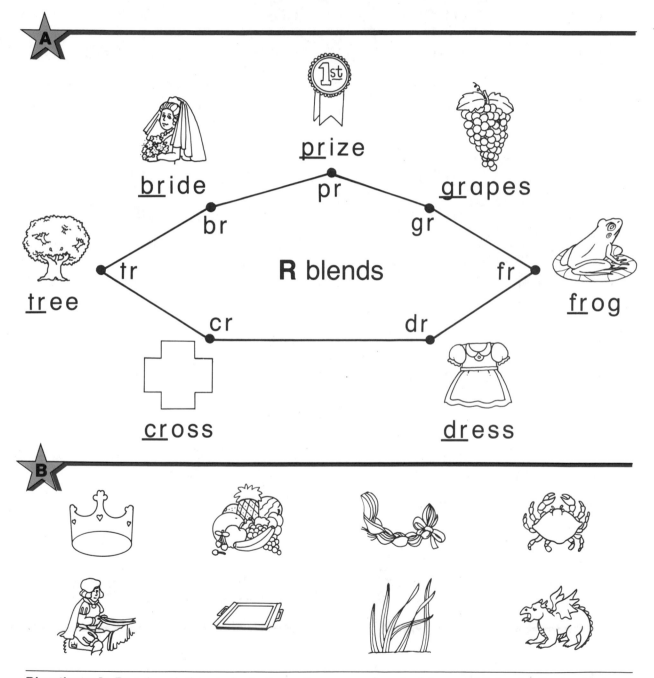

prize

bride   pr   grapes

br   gr

tree   tr   **R** blends   fr   frog

cr   dr

cross   dress

B

Directions: In Part A, ask the students to say the name of each picture and listen for the beginning blend. Then help them match each picture in Part A with a picture in Part B whose name begins with the same blend.

grin grade grass gray	cream crib creep crease
freeze frost free frame	prize pride press praise
dream drapes drove drop	brave brain brick broke
tray trap treat trip	crow crab cross cream

brake	froze	creek	praise
green	treat	drum	trade

Directions: Have the students say each picture name and listen for the beginning blend. Then ask them to read the words in each box and identify the word that names the picture. Challenge them to read the words at the bottom of the page and use each one in a sentence.

LESSON 104: **R** blends

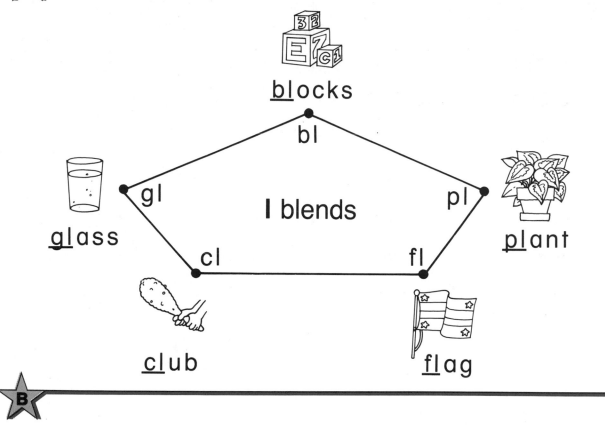

blocks

bl

gl

l blends

pl

glass

plant

cl

fl

club

flag

Directions: In Part A, have the students say the name of each picture and listen for the beginning blend. Help them match each picture in Part A with a picture in Part B whose name begins with the same blend.

LESSON 105: **L** blends

glass globe glove grass	flat flip float flake
plum plant please plate	clam clap class clock
blame blob blade brake	fly flame flea flag
please play plan plane	glaze glad glue grab

blue	plane	flat	black
clay	glue	clue	plan

Directions: Tell the students to say each picture name and listen for the beginning blend. Then have them read the words in each box and identify the word that names the picture. Challenge them to read the words at the bottom of the page and use each one in a sentence.

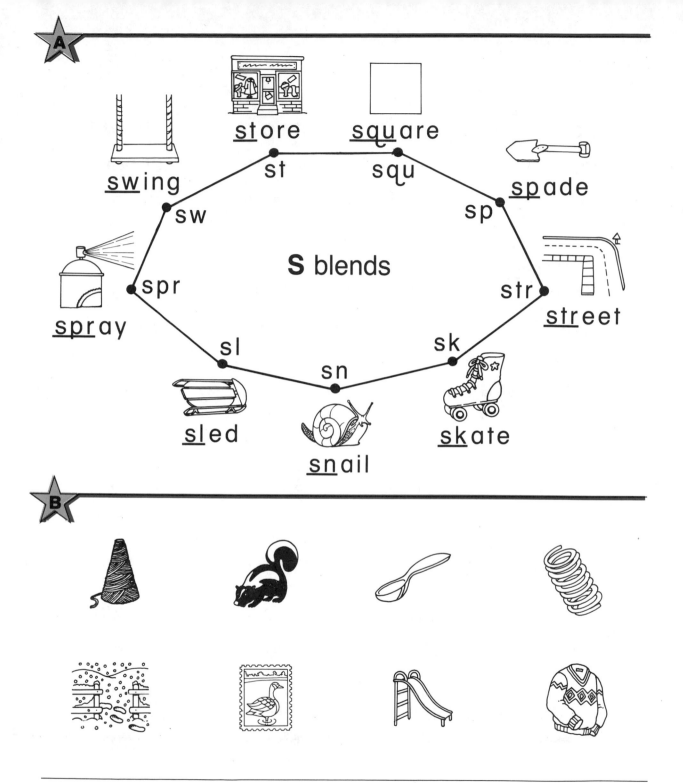

A

swing — sw

store — st

square — squ

spade — sp

S blends

spray — spr

street — str

sled — sl

snail — sn

skate — sk

B

Directions: In Part A, have the students say the name of each picture and listen for the beginning sound. Help them match each picture in Part A with a picture in Part B whose name begins with the same blend.

LESSON 107: **S** blends

strap street	snip sneeze
slate stream	snow sneak
skip skate	state stem
skin skull	stop steps
sway swell	scram spray
slip swim	spring sprung
spoke span	squid square
spend spin	squeeze spare

steam	spin	strike	skin
snap	slope	sprain	swan

Directions: Have the students say each picture name and listen for the beginning blend. Then ask them to read the words in each box and identify the word that names the picture. Challenge them to read the words at the bottom of the page and use each one in a sentence.

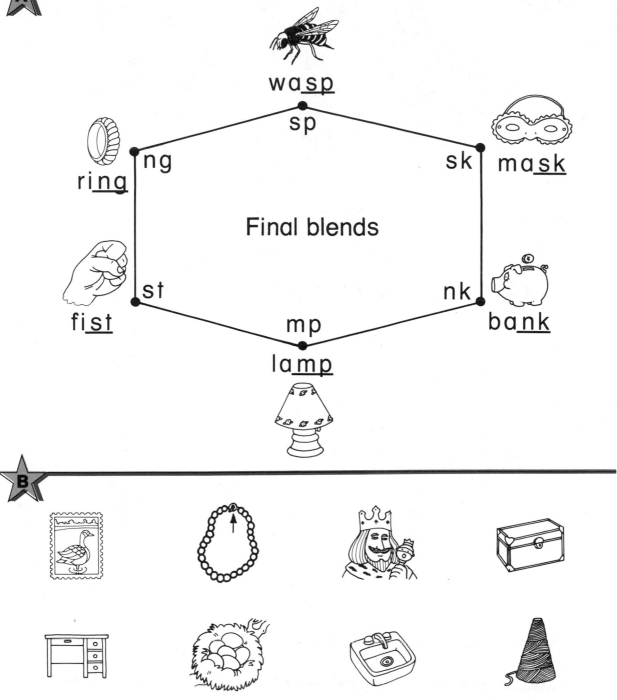

wa**sp**

sp

ng
ri**ng**

sk ma**sk**

Final blends

st
fi**st**

nk
ba**nk**

mp
la**mp**

Directions: In Part A, have the students say the name of each picture and listen for the ending blend. Help them match each picture in Part A with a picture in Part B whose name ends with the same blend.

LESSON 109: Final blends

113

The black dress has a ring of red on the sleeve.

1. Please close the drapes near the sink.
2. Let Frank sleep at his desk.
3. Bren can glue the globe but not the mask.
4. A brave king will send the plane home.
5. We can use soap to clean the brass tray.
6. Glenn broke the clock and the screen.
7. Brad will be fast as he prunes the plum trees.
8. A wasp was on the jay's wing.

1. Fred likes to swing on the oak trees.
2. The class will clean the desks.
3. A skunk is black and has stripes.
4. Please do not slip on the wet street.
5. The bank will close at five.
6. Fran likes to slide fast on the sled.
7. We will clap if Clem puts on his mask.
8. The blue and green flag waves in the breeze.

Directions: Have the students read each sentence aloud and identify the blend words.

 pon<u>y</u>

 fl<u>y</u>

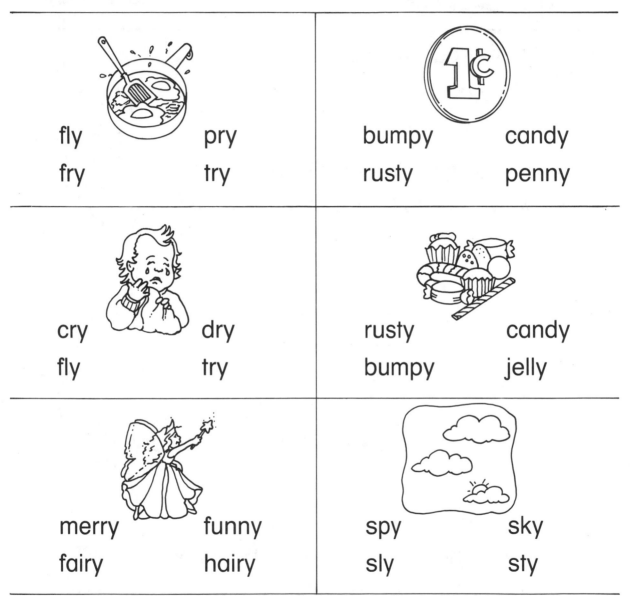

fly	pry
fry	try

bumpy	candy
rusty	penny

cry	dry
fly	try

rusty	candy
bumpy	jelly

merry	funny
fairy	hairy

spy	sky
sly	sty

Directions: Tell students to say each picture name and listen for the sound of **Y**. Then have them read the words in each box and identify the word that names the picture.

Teddy's pet piggy is in the sty.

B

1. My pet bunny is silly.
2. It is a hot, dry, and windy day.
3. Try to fly the kite up in the sky.
4. Polly will try to ride the pony.
5. Sally likes to fry meat for the puppy.
6. Teddy is not happy on rainy days.
7. Try to pry the lid off the empty can.
8. I gave the rusty pail to Dotty.

C

1. Is Puffy a funny name for a kitty?
2. I will give Peggy a penny for the lily.
3. Bobby did not like to see the baby cry.
4. Tammy can see gulls in the sky.
5. Harry will not fry the meat.
6. Randy has a lucky penny to spend.
7. The baby likes my silly games.
8. The road by my home is sandy and bumpy.

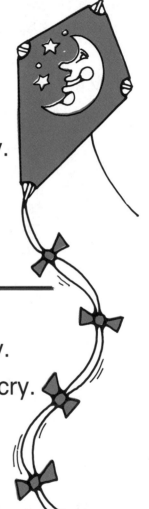

Directions: Have the students read each sentence aloud and identify the words containing the long **I** or long **E** vowel sound of **Y**.

LESSON 112: **Y** as a vowel

Word Endings, Consonant Digraphs, and Contractions

A

ed as **ed**	ed as **t**	ed as **d**
seat	kick	sail
seat<u>ed</u>	kick<u>ed</u>	sail<u>ed</u>

B

rented	bumped	played
needed	huffed	spelled
ended	tacked	mailed
melted	dressed	rained

C

1. Greg painted my rusty bike.

2. We floated on the stream on my raft.

3. Patsy mailed the box to Freddy.

4. Blake's cut healed in four days.

5. Joan helped us tack the rug.

6. Randy washed and pressed the black suit.

7. Lee rocked and patted the baby to sleep.

8. Mom brushed and braided Jan's hair.

Directions: In Part B, have the students read each word and identify the sound of the ending **ed**. Then tell them to read the sentences in Part C and identify each word with an **ed** ending.

LESSON 113: Inflectional ending **ed**

spelling waiting playing sailing

drying frying eating loading

picking rocking drinking filling

B

1. Jeff is training his dog to do tricks.

2. Mom is peeling the beets at the sink.

3. Sue is rocking the baby to sleep.

4. Fran was kicking the ball.

5. Flying a box kite is lots of fun.

6. The plane is landing on the grass.

7. If it is raining, we will not go.

8. I liked the ending of the poem best.

C

1. We passed the day boating on the lake.

2. Melting ice makes a real mess.

3. Dad is fixing and painting Ben's bike.

4. Fred is waiting to be seated.

5. Mom is dressing the baby in a red suit.

6. We played in the foaming waves at the beach.

7. Jean is filling the pail as we sail.

8. It was raining as the club hiked up the hill.

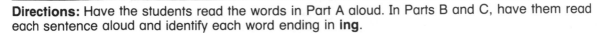

Directions: Have the students read the words in Part A aloud. In Parts B and C, have them read each sentence aloud and identify each word ending in **ing**.

<u>th</u>is

<u>th</u>umb

pa<u>th</u>

them	thank	bath
then	think	with
those	thing	teeth
this	thump	cloth
that	thin	fifth
take	top	tune
tenth	tie	met
wait	tire	boat

C

1. The three thin cats needed a bath.
2. Thank that man for the pretty cloth.
3. Do not thump on the tenth desk.
4. Those mules have big teeth.
5. That baby has a sore throat.

Directions: In Part B, ask the students to read each word and tell whether it contains a **t** or **th** sound or both. Have them identify the sound of the digraph **th**. Then have them read the sentences in Part C and identify each word with the **th** digraph.

<u>wh</u>ale

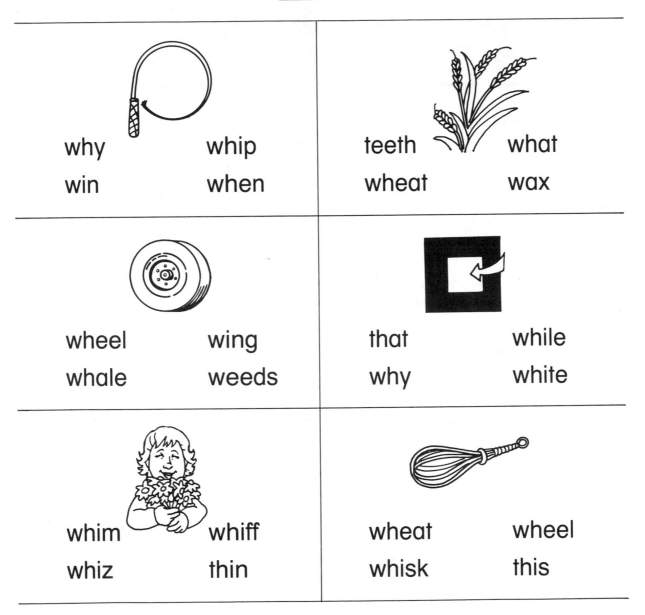

why whip win when	teeth what wheat wax
wheel wing whale weeds	that while why white
whim whiff whiz thin	wheat wheel whisk this

Directions: Have the students say each picture name and listen for the consonant digraph **wh**. Then tell them to read the words in each box and identify the word that names the picture.

LESSON 116: Consonant digraph **wh**

 <u>sh</u>ip

 di<u>sh</u>

fell shore	sail shut
she shell	shoe ship
fresh fish	shelf shine
flash fist	sheep shell
shade shape	wish with
fame shake	whip wash

Directions: Tell the students to say each picture name and listen for the consonant digraph **sh**. Then have them read the words in each box and identify the word that names the picture.

LESSON 117: Consonant digraph **sh**.

121

 <u>ch</u>ain

 pea<u>ch</u>

chum	church
chest	clock

math	match
mats	map

chip	chop
chime	chin

reach	beach
beak	cube

late	catch
lunch	rich

cheese	check
clean	cheap

Directions: Tell the students to say each picture name and listen for the digraph **ch**. Then have them read the words in each box and identify the word that names the picture.

LESSON 118: Consonant digraph **ch**

Three whales chased a ship near shore.

1. We must rush to get the wheat to the mill.

2. I brush my teeth three times a day.

3. Which way did the sheep run?

4. Thad has a big scratch on his chin.

5. We must rush to catch the ship.

6. Please get change at the bank.

7. Do not let the baby grab the cheese.

8. We ate the peach in the dish.

1. It is cheap to eat fish at the shore.

2. In the play, the watch was shut in the chest.

3. Try to reach the chain on the door.

4. We reached the path to the beach.

5. This cloth will match my dress.

6. We will sit in the shade while Mom shops.

7. Nell and the chum wore matching charms.

8. Why did the bunny thump its feet?

Directions: Have the students read the sentences aloud and identify the words containing consonant digraphs.

I am = I'm	can not = can't
she is = she's	does not = doesn't
he is = he's	is not = isn't
it is = it's	will not = won't

B

1. She's watching the whales.
2. I can't fix this watch.
3. The men won't fish for bass.
4. It's time to go to lunch.
5. This cloth isn't white, it's blue.

C

1. <u>She</u> <u>is</u> sitting on the bench.
2. That clock <u>does</u> <u>not</u> run late.
3. <u>He</u> <u>is</u> going to ride the mule.
4. That duck <u>will</u> <u>not</u> bite.
5. Nick <u>does</u> <u>not</u> use those skates.
6. Jan <u>will</u> <u>not</u> dive in the pond.
7. <u>It is</u> sad that you <u>can</u> <u>not</u> go.
8. <u>I am</u> sorry <u>he</u> <u>is</u> ill.

Directions: In Part A, ask the students to read the words and the contractions. In Part B, tell the students to read the sentences aloud and identify each contraction. Then have them read the sentences in Part C. Ask them to replace the underlined words with the contraction.

End-of-Book Review

freeze	quit	vote	reach
drop	which	camp	prize
huff	skate	box	luck
oak	sack	kept	gift
peach	track	grape	sweet

block	pump	breeze	these
float	fly	laid	shine
hug	wire	must	baby
pry	suit	slide	aim
quick	rock	them	fuzz

gray	coast	silk	pay
mix	real	ask	mix
print	why	drum	zone
queen	pet	glue	shake
door	sneeze	dear	cuff

Directions: Have the students read each word aloud and use it in a sentence.

Crabs can swim deep in the sea.

---

1. Sue got a bump on the cheek and chin.
2. Those wheels go on my red bike.
3. We can't snap the screen door shut.
4. Cathy spilled milk on the road map.

5. Clem will dust and clean the clock.
6. It isn't time to go.
7. Please meet us at the docks.
8. Nine mules left the dusty path.

---

1. The king sat on his grand throne.
2. Pat put three plums on my plate.
3. Leave the glove on his desk.
4. Josh ate eggs, toast, and fish.
5. The black bug got free from its box.

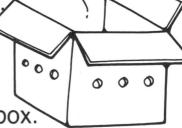

6. Can't Teddy pry the lid off this can?
7. It is fun to try to flip stones in the pond.
8. Tammy won't drive too fast on this bumpy road.

Directions: Have the students read each sentence aloud.

End-of-Book Review

We can make capes from this cloth.

1. This cute cup broke when it fell.
2. A fox likes to chase my bunny.
3. That mule may kick if Bill tries to pet it.
4. Dad pruned the plum trees last month.
5. Cheese and dates make a great snack.
6. Three fat frogs sat on lily pads.
7. I lost the key and can't get in the door.
8. We will reach the beach at five.

---

1. Abby lay in the hay and watched the sky.
2. Pal cut his leg on the wire by the road.
3. I owe Mom the cash from the sale.
4. He's waiting to see Bren skate.
5. My milk spilled on the red rug.
6. We must mail this box by six.
7. She's going to paint with the big brush.
8. Don't kick the ball or it will pop.

Directions: Have the students read each sentence aloud.